The Island Rescu

William Palmer's poems and short stories have appeared in
many magazines and have been broadcast.
He is the author of six novels, the most recent being
The India House, (Jonathan Cape, 2005).
In 1997 he was awarded the Travelling Scholarship of the Society
of Authors. He is at present a
Royal Literary Fund Writing Fellow
at the University of Warwick.

BY THE SAME AUTHOR

WILLIAM PALMER

The
Island
Rescue

The MELOS Press

First published in 2007 by The Melos Press,
38 Palewell Park, London SW14 8JG

ISBN 978-0-9555157-0-5

A catalogue record for this book is available from
the British Library

Printed and bound in Great Britain by
Smith Settle, Yeadon, West Yorkshire

ACKNOWLEDGEMENTS

Acknowledgements are due to the following publications
in which some of these poems
first appeared:

Anvil New Poets, The Keats-Shelley Review, London Magazine, Poetry Review, The Rialto, The Shop, and *Stand Magazine*

'The Storm' first appeared in *Mandeville's Home Truths*
published by Mandeville Press.
'The Exhumation of Lizzie Siddal' was written for the
opening of an exhibition of the paintings of Dante Gabriel Rossetti
at the Barber Institute, University of Birmingham, in 2003.

A group of these poems was awarded the Collection Prize at the
Listowel Writer's Week festival in 2006

Thanks are due to The Ireland Funds for
financial assistance in producing this book,
and to the Listowel Writers' Week for all of their help.

CONTENTS

I

II

III

I

THE STORM

Toasts to 'the guarantors of order'
proceed all night behind high and golden curtains.
Snow lolls on the forest branches; along the mountains
arcs flare huge silhouettes across the border.

All night the solitudes build in and out;
our bed reflected through the alders' rout.
The land outside moves, is a land awake.
Moons in our windows mould and break.

The sill still ticking with last night's thaw,
but slower – tonight we heard the winds and saw
all outside confuse and storm.
About one and the air is suddenly warm,

with snow falling. I dreamt,
you say, the storm took off our roof:
above, stars shone brilliant, cold, aloof;
the road light leant in and wept.

THE AMERICAN

I

Let whisky ease the mood
– though the whole bottle, glancing white,
eventually announces only
contents of the table – words, words
and the idly unpolished wood.

'Presumptive elegies, spectra
the stars unfold invisibly...'
One by one the radio
numbs its stations; the night
grumbles with flights to Arcadia

less and less... I hold
your fabulous republic;
the crumpled mountains
slanting down, the cloud that sits
high always above the mild

smiles, in what was cold?
what was hot? for that stilled sepia land
– the tame fox of your father, the frame house
they stood before – your brother, sisters,
my grandmother with child

– you...

2

'Grandfather sold pianos on the Indian reservation.'
Quick talking, energetic, in black-tubed
trousers. Then his watch-chain swung
above the leaning hull,
the warm, amniotic cabins

phosphored and starred interchangeably,
to England. To the blue lawns of the big house
your childhood knew; the maids and motor;
the poor relations bumming in the hall
- till the next escape across the sea.

You dwelt in Paradise until he left at last,
not to return — 500 sovereigns in a Gladstone bag,
not his — our family a nest of thieves
and drunkards suddenly; a Miltonic fall
retold by some dim novelist.

3

That was worse for you — not knowing
how your father ended: immortal, unimpoverished,
forever setting forth — the huge ship
not larger than his hope, the sea amoral, diamond
succeeding diamond day, and darkness waiting

unfulfilled... And now I meet it
in remembering:
night conjures a trip
across the Mawddach estuary
— my father in the middle of the ferry row-boat,

his hat pushed back, Lear of the Suburbs,
his rage on holiday.
How does he look at us – his sons?
Telling again the story of his gilded father;
how he would never leave us

like that, oh, marvellous man. He turns his face
to the horizon - suddenly far.
The boat grounding, he rises, stumbles
– Something I've lost, and it evades me like the sea
moulded around his trailing fist, a travelling space...

THE MAP OF LOVE

The glass comes dry
just after rain
the roofs dry
blue, grey-blue and grey.

The gold clocks hiss
before they chime;
an island echoes
off the bay...

The chart returns
by woods in fall,
bears trees as ferns.
The meadows walk

in green and rise
in finger-
prints of giants
whorled.

Blue water's
paper on the bed,
your island white
its river red...

The estuary's white
tower lays down
a shadow to water
earth will turn

over the drowned
light-streaming town.

THE TYRANNY OF I

Do you remember the story of poor Mishka?
Mishka, who read his creation,
full of nicotine, wine and passion,
to Babel – and it was worthless,

second-hand – a thousand hands
had done the thing before – and will do.
My room was long and slanted to the window.
If I came in too drunk I would disturb

myself by walking into the ceiling,
which would heave up, absorbent with its rot.
All day I would go out and did not.
The room below made love, then slept.

Evening all afternoon, and then the real evening
came down. Words, wine and snow.
The local moon shone on my narrow
desk, telling the moon, again, that it existed.

'His fingers are fat as grubs.'
(from Mandlestam's poem on Stalin)

I am the only thing that you fear.
All night the temperature falls;
stars break at last
into three o'clock, tree-brakes separate
in moonlight, and two badgers pass
over the empty road.

Your hands are raised, the lamp casts them far.
They move on the still,
blue faces of portraits,
papered walls. Silence leans as you lean;
a black cabinet disclosed by one curtain,
night defaced, unpeaceful.

The negroes at the barber's
face the light, that comes,
that takes a white square
church, turns it to a monument.

The child with the little cock
who dare not take
a step for fear of falling
– hands reach out – has

already seen the pictures perched
about the fireplace, birds searched
for in the trees and shot down, that
the light is everywhere.

Charms
and birdscares on the telephone wires;
forks; grandmother's photo and black Fords;
a note on the fireplace – 'Please be Quite…'

dyslexia of dialect, despair;
the harness hung on the open door.

THE WATER STEPS

1

Memory is water, broaching reason.
In winter the boating lake rocks
under its ice meniscus,
thin lapping across the top step,
overflows to a railed culvert,
goes under the road, car wheels,
park signs, to a tangle
of overgrowth, railed again,
turns, runs aside from the grey, mock,
solid-funnelled Sea Cadets' ship
flat bottomed and grounded in frost.

2

From Easter to Easter my father travels.
From the first paleness and resting,
his head turned away on the pillow,
- a year from the drought – 'Oh,
I am tired' – the pink, furrowed brow
impatiently weaving
from light to shadow.

3

From lover to lover,
exchanging cries –
'Ah, see the birds that dip and hover,'
in the words of one
to the mouth of another.

The gulls fly through
the Border Bridge below.

Clear waters
into a dirty sea
decant our vows. Starboard,
the stars begin to travel with me.

The town slides off.
Dusk follows the train south.

4

Easter. A christening.
A lit candle over
the child's squalling brow.
whose eyes, unpouched,
relentlessly search
the vaulted ceiling for the source
of water, flame,
the heavy, hanging air.

5

Water is memory...
At the water steps standing
in summer, or sprung winter, at this Easter,
each rope and torque of water
- as if struggling to hold irreconcilables
they struggle together, are
forever joined, and fall – arguing like angels.

LETTERS

'...in the cool villas
the writers argue all day
on money and art,
the fled city,
gods left behind,
the rate of interest,
the radical...
the bourgeoisie...'

The land is late.
The land is lying in wait.

'The plough we bought it seems
is not the right kind.
Or the land is wrong.
Tomorrow we drive to Babylon
for seed and fuel,
and wine and, hopefully, some grass...'

The woods draw near.
The woods are growing very queer.

'Well, if you're going in, please ask,
how long have we been here,

how long we have to stay?'

THE BURNING BOOK

Severed from sleep,
an axe's wound in wood,
the letter V,
illuminated blue, pictures
hierarchies of a simple god:

the clear heart of the forest,
cut apart, displays
unstartled hares
by sun, striped deer
in milky shadow,
and few, huge, above the clearing's stare,

stars in the day, white doves stopped in the air.

Below the overhanging trees,
two naked lovers
— across the page the hunters come;
the birds fly fearfully out of cover.

THE MIRROR OF THE DOVE

Like lovers to
their sudden futures,
under Mill Bridge
the seamless waters
part, the Dove in two:

the weir fall-races,
turbulences,
crests, white undersided,
where our faces
cannot show, show

division
undivided – a vision
of the turning mill,
veined water running in
the hollow wheel,

the song's partition; it is still.

Silence between
grace and order, silence between
the arches of air
and water, silence
far falling where,

over the other
arm of the river
that flowing, glistens,
Venus, the lover
of musicians,

makers of words,
dancers, the bird's
stone mouth,
throat flickering, fords
in the South.

THE SEANCE

That lost, dingy kingdom,
un-Babel of the echoes, spotted mirrors,
in the hall the forms of lovers
— coat shadows at the corners of the eye.

'Is the door shut?'
Now look up and search
for silver trumpet, tambourine returns
— unanswered by the crowded flowers on the wall;

the full sky responding only
with its imitative tears,
the known, unechoed music of the rain
— the deft, sad drummer on the window pane.

A FOUND POEM

The Queen is the Prince of Wales.
Ireland is a little town.
A violet is a pretty bird.
A mountain would be on the water.
The sea is made of land.
You can go in a train to America, all the way.
A cow being milked is a lion.
The sun is in the North in the middle of the day.

All go in the pit-hole
where them be buried.
They never get out or live again.
They have not a soul. I have not one.
It's quite an end of people when they die.

The devil is a good person.
Christ was a wicked man.

[All the lines are taken from answers given
in interviews with young factory workers in
Birmingham in the early 1860s, as recorded
in White's *Third Report on the Metal Manufactures
of the Birmingham District, 1864.*]

MR BLUNT'S HISTORY OF ART

We seek them buried
as forefathers
their tragic gestures
and huge humours

grand in war.
The famous princes;
monstrous seraphim;
deserted graces —

their trumpets shine,
soundless; furors
stilled; in heaven holding
quiet guitars…

Pillars candle
in the sun; a statue
rears its head from a well.
What is it to you?

From Leger's Lego stones
shadows fall like shelves,
air makes bones appear
to clean themselves.

Pale clouds sweep
eyes of a sleeping man
— satiate, inconsolable —
— dreaming the barbarian.

EXILES

Up on the hill the convent's broken windows shine
and crows for nuns
stand in the garden's
last reducing snow
where the bare birches rise.

A bird goes up; a solitary cry,
slow flight away —
arrival, parting, silence —
as a hand's last wave from land,
the open mouths along the quay.

THE GOOD SHIP EMPIRE

Here is a ship sailing on a cigar band,
red and gold and

blue the ocean. The captain appears.
He is a particularly hand-
some gentleman,
asking where we

are bound? What particular course we are on?
The crew murmurs. Could it be
— could it? — that the hofficers emselves doan
no the course we is on?

Send out birds, says Leftenant Aubergine.
They will report if the land

is fit to be landed upon.
If the grass rhymes with arse. A man
(like the fist of a ham
his huge head)
mounts the bridge and announces

Sir, we ave run aground…
On the blue-green

rocks. The faces reflected
in the ship's shadow
see, to their chagrin,
how, through their blond-bladed ripples,

the keel of the ship
is eating the sea-green pebbles

like peas on a series
of endless, impossible knives.

THE EXHUMATION OF LIZZIE SIDDAL

A fire is lit beside the grave:
Officers of the Court, the diggers,
the poet's representative, all look in…
The body is raised – and, miracle,

she is quite unchanged. The book wrapped
in her lovely hair is mildewed – and the friend
leans down, weeping, and lifts the book
and, with it, some hair parts from the head.

Oh perfect. Perfect. Trembling, he holds the book.
The coffin lid's replaced: the guide ropes
are let down again, lowering the resealed box
into that damp, rectangular, glistening place.

He clutches the book, the book –
a small, square shape containing words:
the flames, dwindling, gather to one last blaze
and shine and smoulder in her red-gold hair.

THE GREEK LEXICON

To march out one morning
humming a soft tune
the star on the horse's head
above us still, spring rains
muddying the road.

To be decided - whether as tallow
for candles our flesh will be used
to light our enemies' rooms, our bone-
meal to be scattered across their fields.
Or to settle ourselves

in victory, to tell tales
about honour, or be silent.

II

That hollow-cheeked man has been on a mission,
has come back, hardly able to speak.
When given wine

he has started to sing, in a high, false voice
and then to cry,
calling the name of some friend.

III

In our minds to contend with, to desire,
to fight, to make love,

to mean what is lost deep in ourselves,
what we have in the dark before sleep,
with each other, talking together

in the dark there behind us
with its dead tongue.

ORDERS OF THE DAY

Each man will rise
and stand behind his stone.
There'll be no talking
but each of you may stand
at ease, alone.

The frost will lay
a dimly shining white
between each row
of thirteen stones.
It won't be light

for two hours yet.
Wind will blow hard
from the east; sky remain
black, but pierced – so
brilliantly starred.

It won't be until noon
(sun low all day)
when they get from their cars
and feel our cold.
What do they say?

– we cannot hear.
As they walk between
the frosted aisles
along each row of stones,
we will remain unseen.

Some cry; all are moved
by the kind order of stone
and grass, the terse
inscriptions, walls of names...
Then they are gone.

After this short day,
away from village lights,
the long dark fields will wait
where we must settle
for the night.

YOU MUST KNOW EVERYTHING
(The title of a story by Isaac Babel, b. 1894 – executed 1940)

Babel was ashamed, when young,
to admit he knew the names
of none of the singing birds,
or trees, or flowers – and was told:

'A writer must know everything.'
Even, at the end, the numbers stamped
on the pistol's barrel, the zero
of the muzzle

- from which a bird will fly,
a creature with no name,
lost in a dark place, piercing
through voice and memory,

obliterating song.
At last to break, and fall,
spent, into the high-walled yard
of Everything.

But then – to be picked up,
brought to the slanted light,
to flutter and rise again,
the yard floor shadowed

first, then lit by absence, flight.

II

VENUS RISING

At five in the morning the room is cold,
and you, reflector in the small round glass
held between cup and earthenware
in the tenth-hand cabinet,

summon a shuddering
halo in the silver behind the glass,
a ghost to swear
we love, have hope for money, stillness.

As you rise, stall, violet
in the second refraction by glass,
why, through the opened window, do you wear
the look of a stranger as you look back?

DOG DAYS

My dog in the long grass peers at the morning;
that prick of ice on her soft profiled eye
is Sirius
of heat and pain, naked in bed,
troubled by sadness
after anger.

HOSPICE

In this airy bright cool room
– its windows open to the Spring,
two beds, one bare, unoccupied,
one left an hour ago – she reads.

Of the Browning's life in Italy,
the odd, dead, love between them;
their little spaniel dog; their rooms,
still visited by a few it seems.

(For the distanced thrilling
of those two, the views of Venice,
passionate deceit,
imagined voices…)

She smokes a cigarette,
then, dressed in a white gown,
not hers, walks down the short
sun-blooming corridors

to the cold, burning needle
placed to her breast –
in another white, tall room,
with an almost identical view of Spring.

A TRIP TO THE BLIND ASYLUM

(a nineteenth century narrative for a young woman's voice)

1

'Curable – if taken soon enough in hand…'
She took my hand
and led me through the garden
– starting to scent –
handing me up the carriage step
– the coldness of her fingers –
with Henry's hot hand pulling.
Then Mother settling
beside me; beside herself,
not knowing what to say.

2

Now I am taken, feeling
as though I take them
unwillingly, through darkness to darkness.
The world too far, too near
in the feel of the seat, the breathing of Henry,
the start, the heavy ring
of horses' hooves, the brush
of cool air now we are going.
And I am flying through night
on a midsummer morning;
an echoing head; my body
a tadpole's, insignificant,
to be ignored for the present.
A head carried through air,
cutting swiftly through air,
air a felt presence,
a net tightened.

3

Travelling with Henry,
I know he is looking at me
and that he smiles.
All is a thick velvety black
pushed aside in
tiny, exquisite
brilliant corners,
a huge mirror facing the sun,
its back silver finely scratched.
'It's sunny,' says Henry. 'Again.'
'We are passing – oh
such a pretty wood. Oh, I am sorry…'
And I feel Mother move on the seat
in her sorrow.
'Tell me the colours.'
'Green and brown,' says Henry. 'Brown and green.'
Why does he hate me?
Now I shall never see him again.
Mother will die.
And if Henry should visit, he will,
year after year,
bore, go bald,
talk through poor teeth,
mask his voice
with his young face forever.
Now I am glad of this carriage.
It holds me
and Mother and Henry
and the disappeared fields and
all the stopped faces.

Now we are turning.
The sound of the wheels,
rhythm of hooves, changes.
My mother explains the high stone pillars,
iron gates, porticoed house, girls
walking hand in hand
on the straight paths of the garden.
'Miss Race? Mrs Race?'
a neat small
buzzingly ecstatic voice
like a tired bee.
'Yes. Yes?' says my mother.
Another cold hand helps me down.

5

We are mounting steps.
I stumble.
'Take my arm, my dear.'
'No. Thank you.' I will feel the door.
The hard wood rising
cool, with a little smoothed-out
painted-over indentation
where my fingers grip.
It is a liberation you feel
when you know you are here
to be kept.

6

Never to be let go now.
To move in my skull
as freely as the world
this smooth invisible house,
each open window
a square enclosing space;
the warm broad curves of the balustrade.
I have years to learn
these Euclidities of darkness,
the mysteries of dress,
to read by the Moon.

THE EMBARKATION

As the forest falls
the blue lake brightens;
the last, recorded small
creatures scramble ashore.

And we wait – happy
in the evening garden –
our food and drinks laid out,
the games-net spread

taut white, in time,
above the lawn –
but, after this season,
we must also leave.

At the garden's end,
up to the landing, a small
boat is skimming
the blue lake darkening,

the boat nearing faster
the boat that does not
dip in the water
as we step in.

THE ENGLISH LOVERS

Make a cage.
The gate shakes.
Warm my hand.
The hat falls.

He sees me.
He feels wet.
We went to bed.
He fed the bees.

Fire shines.
Vines give wine.
Kites rise to the sky.
Lips are red.
Fir swims.
Birds sing.
Girls spin.
He rides.

He holds the rose to my nose.
The dove took food.

I can tame his bird.
I am not old.
My bird hops on my hand.

The red sun sets.
The moon is white.
This stone feels hard.
Ice makes the hand cold.

It is not safe to play with fire.
There is no harm in the dark.
It is a sin to wish for it.

(A poem made by using unaltered phrases from *Curso de Inglés*, by
Professor H. MacVeigh, published in Madrid in 1888)

THE WIDOWERS

It's three o'clock.

We have outdrunk the whisky
and gone out

to walk the walls
above the estuary.

The tide is out.
Fifty – more – swans sleep

on the water
curved in the milky sands.

The lighthouse flashes far
and on the waters, sand,

the slowed light passes
like a fan.

It is as if we stood
in a great and shadowed hall

whose roof grows light,
while, on the stone-flagged floor,

a slow, meticulous
photographer lays prints,

his squares of silver
forcing ghosts to life.

It's nearly four.

The light fans out,
goes past once more.

THE PRIEST OF DREAMS

He rises as the birds
take shape and call
(you could not call it
singing at that hour).
Coffee and bread;

he reads, light-headed,
from the saints – all those
uninnocent, other men
– until the trees unshroud
and stand about.

His mind sways with visions:
of a blue mountain;
fountains at the ends of streets;
the lover, unchanging,
in the gradual garden.

Light fills his day
unsimply one end to the other.
The blue mountain lifts
into each brilliant tomorrow
attempted burials of sorrow.

In all these holy, invented hours,
the fountains play, whose waters
– promised not to fail – fall and fall,
empty their stars,
becoming days.

WHAT TIME IS IT?

On the pear tree at six
the blackbird speaks.

He talks of no creation
that we, translated to his garden

and looking back, could ever see. I go inside.
The back door has the same, jarring slide.

Again, against the quiet, I rage.
You sit, forever reading the same page

at the table just behind me.
You listen once more, patiently,

to my ideas of Time. The world ever Present;
Past and Future irredeemably absent;

this room a delusion – what is out of sight
simply chaos, juggling light...

'Yes, love. But...' I sit. In a moment I'll turn,
and the past turn

with me, and you will not be there
nor will be, smiling into the darkening air.

THE AVENUE

Always, in mine, by some
interior daylight
the dreams take place:
never by night

those insufficient conversations,
intricate and strange
cities, dull rooms, unfinished
poems, snatches of music,

recurring doorways, steps, sharp-
shadowed arches, tiled
towers, the joyful dogs
of childhood...

The closest I have come
to dreaming of the dark
is when you walked
in that lime avenue.

It's dusk. You halt
and smile uncertainly,
as if we were meeting,
both a little early,

and I wake, weeping.

LETTER TO MY DAUGHTER

The hare limped trembling through the frozen grass...

These words of Keats — the animal moving
through the vowels,
the consonants that stand
as frosted blades, or emptied trees

— I cannot give you any more than these —
or, better — share them with you.
Their tenderness may make amends
for those harsh speeches, quickly uttered,

that seem to wither up the earth.
Our lives, our words —
they are the same. The one good gift
I'd give to you is knowing always

what I haven't always known myself
— that what's not given can never be returned,
that words not given when they're sought
limp, tremble, rot into a frozen ground.

AFTER THE BAR

What is he doing here,
the simplest, most complex god
transmuting the air
around you to the most odd

blue you have ever seen?
It is the smoke from ten cigarettes
floating in front of a screen
on which the facial aggregates

of the crowd at the bar
approach, recede, talk
in the slurred, near, clear, and far
voices of strangers. Walk.

As you stir, come about, grind
into the world, from sleep you find
those pieces of gravel in your palm are the city,
your hand sparkles in the empty city.

BACH IN THE CONGO

[The Harpsichord and Violin Sonatas...
some critics, including Schweitzer, believe
these pieces were written in mourning,
after the death of Maria Barbara, Bach's
first wife.]

The lamp burns with a flaring wick,
the spirit blemishing blue-yellow
through the bleared, thick

chimney window. The score is spotted,
front cover swollen with the damp;
the one below has rotted

clean away...

This music is not telling
whether it was written
in some forlorn, sweating

forest of the spirit, where
pain burns stubbornly
into pain – defective fire –

or, at an open window say,
was cast over the calm German plain;
another task, allotted for the day.

The notes, suspended, fall

and spire. The crow-quills pluck:
the fiddle soars and ploughs;
its solitary, gouging ache

performing largos, allegros,
adagios, allegros again
and again to those,

to one who will not come again.

ALL SOULS NIGHT

Tonight we all come crowding in,
shaking the snow from coats and hair;
we've come together now so far

that there's no need for names (or fire,
or bread and wine laid out for us)
as we greet each cold newcomer.

Many I haven't seen for years,
and hardly recognise myself
when those old photographs are dealt:

summer again; hands shade our eyes
to stare into the camera's dark.
The window joins a frame to night.

We cannot stay. Holding his tears,
our host moves through us like a ghost.
He draws the curtains, locks the doors.

'Safe home,' we call. 'Safe home, my dears.'

III

THE ISLAND RESCUE

I

He had learned, almost,
to live with it at last:
the lack of noise; no cars
or planes – the curse
of other people
lifted. And those double
columns of time
that marched in a line
to the hill's horizon,
almost invisible...

Oh, there were pubs and bars
– empty, of course.
Those twin-regarding liars,
opening and closing hours,
the only regulation.
Nature, but no Man.
One white road connected all
the red hamlets of the isle.
In the brick villas
stood handless clocks, empty mirrors...

For others had been here
before him: the odd hair
on the back of a chair;
once a cache of photographs
(those never folded griefs) –
boy on an ancient beach,
girl under an apple tree

— then the black and white
give way to colour and new life.
Children. The children grow.
The couple age. Then only one is shown.

What else? Books by the handsome dead:
they mostly went unread.
The houses tidy, gardens neat:
tended in the night
perhaps – he never saw the work
although he woke
at three each morning,
waking to listen again
through the dark's low monotones
of owls and rain
to that more terrible silence.

II

One year, out of some broken clocks,
rabbits' guts, a rusting truck
he managed to construct
a band of four automata,
intended to play the later
– maybe – Beethoven quartets.
Overwound, they sprang to bits.
Nothing he could do. Sadly,
he gathered them piece by piece
and cast them adrift,
using their bandstand as a raft.

When the wind some evenings
moved through their strings,

he heard their distant whines
and jangles; the ragged tones
of incompetent art
— until they drifted out.
So that was it.
Little music, few words,
the wind, waves, singing birds.
Terror at night; and in the day,
drink. Just one companion,
Loss, that almost ghost
which never went away.

But it was those
— the broken castaways —
who brought the stranger here.
A speck between sea and air.
Then three white sails,
their curved triangles
bringing Time in their nearing,
nearing, so slow, so slow, until
— sails drooping, wind gone still —
into the harbour
sailed his future.

III

Its crew had heard
the distant discord
of those broken Sirens.
After the silence
of the blue chart
(a tiny model inching forward),
Captain Kind, First Mate True,

sailors Beauty, Hour-Blue,
and their one (female) passenger,
all blessed what they saw.

She looked to the landfall
(eyes hazel, of wood and hill);
the harbour opened, she could see
a single figure on the quay...
And so they met,
on the wooden, sloping deck,
the stationary islander
and the lovely traveller.
Oh, would she stay?
Would he go with her?

Only one answer...
The island mourns him for a day,
then mirrors and doorways
wash his image clear,
the birds compose one song,
sing it, the grass springs
back where he has stepped,
the island sets itself
for its next guest
– and, far, far out

the land's last gulls
turn back, the ship dwindles
into that starry, rocking west
where lovers, embracing,
take their rest.